THE RCMP MUSICAL RIDE

MAXWELL NEWHOUSE

TUNDRA BOOKS

Published in Canada by Tundra Books,
481 University Avenue, Toronto, Ontario M5G 2E9

Published in the United States by Tundra Books of Northern New York,
P.O. Box 1030, Plattsburgh, New York 12901

Library of Congress Control Number: 2003112846

National Library of Canada Cataloguing in Publication

Newhouse, Maxwell

    The RCMP Musical Ride / Maxwell Newhouse.

ISBN 0-88776-683-8

    1. Royal Canadian Mounted Police–Performances. 2. Royal Canadian Mounted
Police–History. 3. Musical rides (Horsemanship)–Canada. I. Title.

HV8158.7.R69N49 2004   363.2'0971   C2003-905461-6

The publisher extends sincere appreciation to the RCMP for their cooperation
and enthusiasm.

We acknowledge the financial support of the Government of Canada through the Book
Publishing Industry Development Program (BPIDP) and that of the Government of
Ontario through the Ontario Media Development Corporation's Ontario Book Initiative.
We further acknowledge the support of the Canada Council for the Arts and the
Ontario Arts Council for our publishing program.

Medium: Oil on canvas

Printed in Hong Kong, China

1 2 3 4 5 6   09 08 07 06 05 04

To my daughter, Nicole, and her horse, Trooper

Acknowledgments

Thanks to Brad Turner for his support, and a very special thanks to Kathy Lowinger.

Y ou can feel them almost before you see them. The earth trembles as thirty-two great black horses thunder across the field, weaving patterns in perfect unison. Their riders are Mounties in bright scarlet, with gleaming lances drawn.

   Horses and riders in a powerful horsey ballet: the RCMP Musical Ride, Canada's symbol and Canada's pride.

The Ride is a tradition that stretches back to the North-West Mounted Police, who rode their rugged horses out onto the wide prairie in 1874 to keep peace as settlers moved west. For thirty years these riders of the plains watched over vast territory, from the Yukon and the Arctic coast to the American border.

The men of the NWMP rode and they rode well. They practised traditional British cavalry drills and lance work on horseback for hours. They showed off their fine horsemanship for the first time at a performance at the Police Barracks in Regina, Saskatchewan in 1887.

The NWMP have become the Royal Canadian Mounted Police, and they no longer use horses in their day-to-day police work. But the Ride is a splendid way to honor the past. Each year thousands of people watch the Ride in hundreds of towns around the world.

The RCMP Musical Ride's sleek black horses – striking against the red serge jackets of their riders – are spectacularly athletic, agile, and smart. The RCMP raises its own horses, bred for their shiny black coats (only 5 percent of all horses are black); for their power; for their size from sixteen to seventeen hands and 1,200 to 1,400 pounds; and for their calm friendly natures. Each horse has to be able to get along with other horses and crowds of people, and endure hard training and thousands of miles of travel each year.

There are usually ninety-six horses at the stables, including the young horses in training. The horses in the Ride vary from six to twenty-four years.

All the foals born in a particular year have names that begin with the same letter of the alphabet. The next year, the next letter is used. Exceptions are made for the letters Q, U, X, Y, and Z.

Training begins the day a horse is born. Each newborn foal is watched closely. Will it have the right size, the shape, the alertness to join the Ride? The trust between human and horse grows as the foals are handled kindly and gently.

Until they are six years old, young horses are called remounts. There is so much for them to learn: rhythm, voice commands, the way the saddle feels on their back, and the way the bit feels in their mouth. After three years, six to fifteen remounts are chosen to go into training to be part of the Ride.

The first stage of training, lasting from spring to fall, is "working from the ground" or "lunging." A horse, attached to a lunge line by the trainer, is worked on a ten- to twelve-meter circle to give the horse confidence, balance, strength, and to develop obedience. The horse learns to adapt to its saddle so that it can move forward and straight, both walking and trotting.

In the winter, the horses train inside and learn the beginnings of cavalletti – a series of timber jumps that are adjustable in height. When spring comes again, the training becomes progressively more difficult. The horses learn new paces and how to cope with strange objects or noises. After a six-week summer pasture break, the heavy-duty schooling starts: jumping, lateral work, and flexion. The horses also learn the collected canter and trot.

The most important lessons of all have to do with staying calm, no matter how large the crowd or loud the traffic, calm no matter who is in the audience – even the Queen.

All the members of the Ride are full-time policemen and policewomen. When they begin training, they may not know how to ride but they must have at least two years of active police work under their belt. Every year several hundred officers apply, but only 28 are chosen for the two five-week basic training courses in Ottawa. Of those, 14 go on to train for eight more months. They will take on this special duty for three years, and then return to regular police work.

The riders look after their horses, cleaning their stalls and grooming them with a series of brushes, as often as two to four times a day. They clean out their hooves, and even wash their faces.

The spit-and-polish equipment, with its cavalry roots, is part of the pomp and history of the Ride. There's a double bridle because the rider has more control with one hand. The rider sits in a combination dressage / jumping saddle, with long flaps. Look for a white rope around the horse's neck – a head rope that used to be for tying horses, but is now part of the ceremonial tack.

Under the saddle is a blanket or cloth called a Shabracque. And though the markings on it have changed over the years, it's now a dark blue material, with double yellow piping for the officers and single yellow piping for the regular riders. Each rear corner bears the crest of the RCMP – a fused letter *M* and *P* surmounted by a crown.

Every six to eight weeks, the horses are reshod. Their shoes are often made by the RCMP's own farrier, whose job it is to shoe the horses.

Each rider carries a lance made of bamboo, weighing from 3 to 4 pounds and approximately nine feet long, with a pennon or triangular flag below a twelve and one-half inch chrome-plated steel point. Although the NWMP's lances were never used in war, their pennons were red and white – colors adopted by the RCMP at the same time that Canada chose them as its official colors.

Finally, the maple leaf is applied with a stencil on the rump of every horse just before each show.

There have been many horse stars in the Ride, but the most famous of all was Lucky II. For most of his twenty-nine years, Lucky was the lead charger of the Ride, and he met thousands of happy fans throughout his long career. Everywhere he went, he was dignified and friendly.

In Lucky's memory, the RCMP began a wall of honor in the Mounted stables. Lucky's name is the first on that special wall.

Travel is part of the lives of the riders and the horses. There are long, tiring bus trips for the riders to as many as 90 to 150 performances each season. The horses travel by truck, twelve in each.

As soon as they all arrive, the bustle begins: the riding surfaces are prepared; the boots and leather and chrome are polished; the stalls and bedding and tack boxes are set.

The Ride has acted as escort at events such as Queen Victoria's Diamond Jubilee procession in 1897 to the Rose Bowl Parade in Pasadena; from the Lord Mayor's Parade in London, England to the Canada Day Parade in Osaka, Japan.

The instructors in the Equitation Branch of the RCMP design the movements based on the need to mobilize a mounted cavalry regiment – single file, half-sections, and sections at trot, canter, and gallop. The lead rider sets the pace and acts as a subtle conductor, with a nod of the head or a movement of the lance.

History's cavalry war cries are now music that ranges from the Beatles to bagpipes – after all, this is a musical ride. The program changes every year, but it always features dazzling footwork. Perhaps the most difficult step is the turnstile, in which two lines of horses revolve through each other in opposite directions. The horses at the center are almost standing still, while the outside ones are cantering and those in between are trotting or walking.

The final charge is always thrilling. Horses and riders love that special moment of power and freedom. The audience is spellbound. Welcome to the Ride!